I HOPE
THIS FINDS YOU

brandon deem

I Hope This Finds You

Copyright © 2022 Brandon Deem

Photos Edited By:
Josh Brown

Formatting Completed By
Violet Lee Xuan Yin

Book Printed By
Amazon Kindle Direct Publishing

First Printing, 2022

www.ChooseU.org

Message To The Reader

I want to start off by saying thank you. Thank you for supporting me and thank you for letting this book fall into your hands. It belongs here, it belongs with you.

I wrote "I Hope This Finds You" as my second book to showcase that beauty can still grow from heartbreak.

On the cover I chose a hand letting go of a paper plane. When you let go of a paper plane, we have no control over where it goes, we just hope that it flies. So, once you let go of that added weight that holds you back from being you, you'll fly, just like that paper plane because a paper plane represents imagination, desire, magic, simplicity and more. It is parts of your journey through life as well as emotions that you are going through or dealing with.

Somewhere in that beautiful heart of yours there is something you long for and I hope this book helps you find it.

You will never be too much for someone
who cannot get enough of you

One day if not already, you're going to meet someone. And they'll find out your favorite food and how you gently sip your coffee because it's too hot. They'll know how your face looks underneath your makeup and how you crave chocolate at random times throughout the day. They'll know the tv shows that make you happy, and how cranky you get when you're tired. They'll understand how you hate the way you look in some photos but how you love to take them anyway. One day, they'll know everything there is to know about you... and they'll love it all

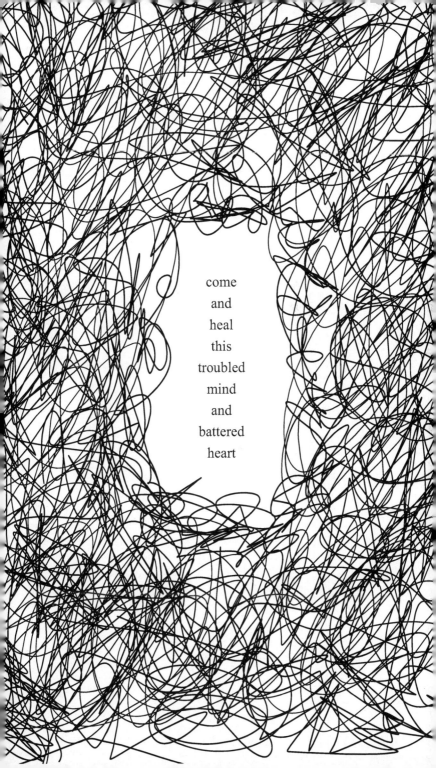

come
and
heal
this
troubled
mind
and
battered
heart

Thanks for loving me
on the days I find it hard to
love myself

don't try harder for someone who doesn't
try at all.

there are too many mediocre things in life,
love shouldn't be one of them.

so, unless it's extraordinary, it's a waste of
your time

Sometimes people come into our lives

not to stay forever.

but to teach us that sometimes things don't

I never wanted to fall in love again
because it seems people only hurt
each other in the end

So, they gave up on you huh?

It's ok because they didn't deserve you anyway.
Your love is like a hurricane, they're used to
playing in puddles. Don't ever apologize for having
too much soul, too much emotion, or too much love
to offer. It's time to let all the toxic shit go & breathe

her voice was the sweetest sound,

but he had selective hearing

In case no one has told you today...
I'm proud of you.
You might not believe it because we've
never met but I'm proud of you because
you are still here today.

I know some days are harder than others
and you want to go and give up. But I'm
proud that you didn't. This world is a better
place because you're in it.
So, if you didn't hear it from anyone else
today, hear it from me

I'm proud of you because you're trying
your best

I
hope
you
find
me
in
your
silent
hours
and
the
crowed
places
we
used
to
go

TIME
IS
PRECIOUS.

If you're not in a good place mentally,
be easy on yourself. Healing is so
different for everyone.
Sometimes it is slow, sometimes it even
feels like you've gone backwards.
But one things for certain, healing has no
time frame so be patient with *yours*.

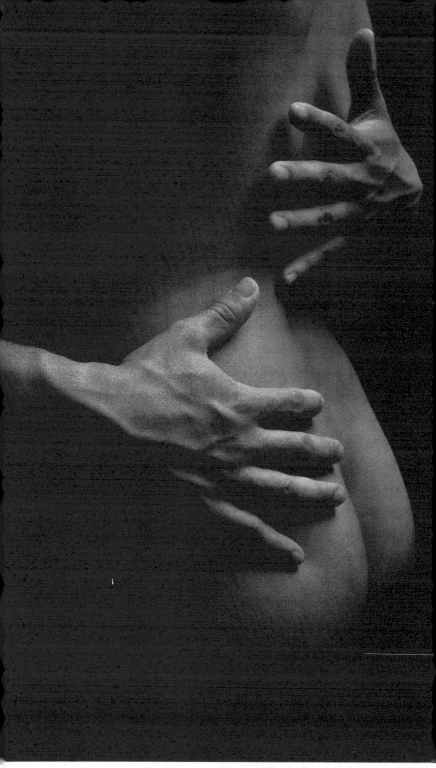

I wanted you in the worst way,
like a smoker wants the last drag from a cigarette,
like the ocean wants to meet the shore,
or like the rain wants to fall.
I wanted you, but wanting you wasn't enough.

I aspired to love everything about her.
Down to every freckle on her face for
they were like beautiful stars dispersed
in the galaxy

If you stay with me, I promise to make you smile everyday with my weird jokes and random kisses.

I promise to hold you when it feels like the world is crashing down on you.

I promise to share my food with you even when you say you're not hungry, but I know you'll still eat a bite.

I will listen to you when you tell me how bad your day was when you come home from work.

If you stay with me, I'll make you see that there are a million reasons to fall for you every day.

sometimes we push people
away just to see if they'll
come back

There's something about late nights in your car when it seems like the rest of the world is asleep. There's a sense of vulnerability when you get in.

It's in the long drives, the parked conversations with friends or lovers, or listening to those songs... you know the one that makes you cry, laugh, or just feel everything.

Late nights in the car are your unofficial therapy sessions and it seems the later at night it gets the further into another world we go. So, I urge you to enjoy the quiet moments and your deep thoughts.

I never knew how
badly I needed you
until I couldn't feel
your warm touch
wrapped tightly
around my tired bones

Maybe I like girls with tan skin and tattoos

Maybe I like girls with broken parts and nothing to lose

Maybe I just like fresh starts

Or maybe I just like warm hearts

Teach me how to
forget about you

the way
you forgot about me

I find myself constantly trying
to find myself. With
untethered thoughts like
waves fighting in the ocean...
both pushing and pulling
finding their way to shore. As I
stumble upon all things I need,
I'm still lost in the emptiness
like the sea. I feel cold air in
my lungs and wind gently on
my fingertips...
but life will always be a
mystery, and there will always
be missing parts of me
scattered on earth I'll never
find like things I couldn't see
standing right in front of me.
What do I believe in?
I don't even think I know
anymore.

Sometimes
all I want to do is
lay in bed and
do nothing with you

I want to love someone new
but it seems
I gave all my loving to you

Reminder

Hey beautiful, Once you start to love yourself it wont matter who doesn't love you

Ok

I didn't fall in love with you because I was
lost or lonely

I fell in love with you because you loved me
when I found it hardest to love myself

I fell in love with you because you gave me
something I've struggled to find in all of the
hearts that I knew before

Loving you comes as easy as breathing to me
And I don't think I'll ever stop

I need to unlearn how to love you.
So I can learn to live without you.

But it's hard to unlove you
because you're what I'm used to

It was there in the silence that I learned
some things are not meant to last.

And he whispered to her ever so
gently as he held her close tightly
wrapped in his arms.
He said

"I just want to love you forever"

TAKE MY HAND
I'LL CALM THE STORM
INSIDE YOUR HEAVY HEART

You know what's crazy,
We never really got to say goodbye. We just
slowly faded until there was nothing left to
hold on to. But I guess that's how life
works, and things go on...but I'd be lying if
I said it never got to me. I mean you were
honestly one of the best things that's ever
happened to me and if fate brings us back
together one day I'll always welcome you
with open arms

She was the closest thing to a wildfire

Igniting every bit of my soul...

and boy did I love to burn for her

I miss you
and I know that I shouldn't
But the hardest part of missing you
Is knowing you still wake up and love things
that aren't me

When you left,
You took a part of me with you,
And I don't know if I'll ever get it back

I DON'T KNOW WHO NEEDS TO HEAR
THIS TODAY BUT
YOU ARE ENOUGH
YOU HAVE ALWAYS BEEN ENOUGH
AND I'M SO SORRY IF THEY EVER
MADE YOU FEEL AS IF YOU WEREN'T
THEY DON'T DESERVE YOU AND THEY
PROBABLY NEVER WILL
IT'S TIME YOU STOP CHASING THOSE
DEAD ENDS AND REMEMBER THAT
YOU DESERVE THE STARS IN THE SKY

I'M A WORK IN PROGRESS
AND
I MIGHT ALWAYS BE
BUT
I'M LEARNING TO BE OK WITH THAT

The problem is...
we stay too long with people
who didn't deserve our heart or a
minute more of our time.
So let them go because you don't
want someone who only gives
you half ass love.

even a blind man
in the black of night
could see the beauty
she radiates

I hope someday you find
a photo of me and maybe
you'll wonder if I still have
that vintage sweatshirt you
loved to wear when it got
cold or maybe you'll
wonder if I still request
pinky promises and maybe
you'll even wonder if I
wonder about you

Your heart was a stormy sea of crashing
waves, capsizing all who ventured there

my favorite part of being in love

is knowing that I get to do it <u>with you</u>

Find someone who
wants to see the world
but also wants to do nothing
on Sunday afternoons.

WE LIVE IN A WORLD WHERE
BROKEN HEARTS STAY BROKEN,
OUR FACES ARE GLUED TO SCREENS,
GAS PRICES ARE TOO DAMN HIGH,
AND THE PEOPLE WHO GIVE THE
BEST ADVICE ABOUT LIFE
ALWAYS SEEM TO STRUGGLE TAKING
THEIR OWN.

You miss them, I know you do. And missing them comes and goes like the ocean tide and right now you're drowning. I'm here to tell you that it gets easier. One day you'll be able to keep your head above the water.

Loving someone with trauma is a forever
journey. It will take resilience and patience
day after day.

Loving them is learning to understand how
they see things differently than you.

At times it's difficult because they have
memories they wish they did not have.
Memories they can't seem to shake no
matter how many years pass from the
incident.

You see, they were ripped apart and stitched
back together with scars to show.

This doesn't make them any less deserving
of love. In fact, they just need a little more
of it.

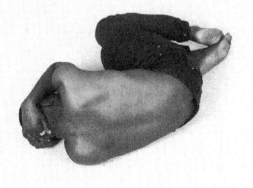

I lost myself in you
in your eyes
in your voice
in the way you said "i love you"

you put

me

through

Hell.

and called

it love

I'm craving something so much deeper
I no longer want small talk anymore.
Tell me more about that scar on your shoulder
you got from falling trying to rollerblade.
Show me your favorite place to go when
you want to disappear from the world.
Call me at 4AM because you want to talk about
your tough relationship with your father.
I want depth because I'm done looking for
permanent homes in temporary people.

You're so used to
seeing your own insecurities,
you don't know how beautiful
you are to a stranger

You know what the fucked-up part is?
You broke me, and with all the pieces still
floating around in my shattered chest,
I still miss you.
I still miss the way you said my name
when you got frustrated with me.
I still miss feeling your warm body pressed
close to mine at night.
I still miss your name showing up on my
phone when you'd call after work.
I still miss you, and I'm trying my hardest
not to.

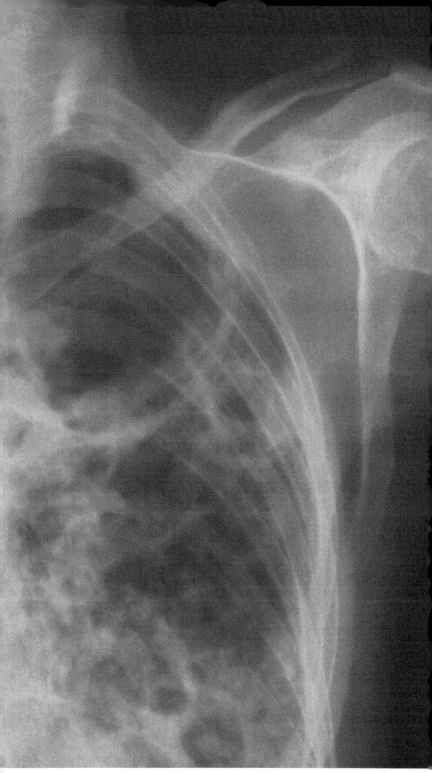

Science says that every 7 to 10 years
your body replaces every cell within.
So until that day, I'll patiently wait until
I have a body that your hands haven't
trapped me in.

– bd // Shedding Skin

Sometimes,
things don't work out
no matter how hard you try to save it.

We made eye contact on your train slowly
passing through the Union Station. We were
just two strangers heading in opposite
directions. However, in that moment, you felt
familiar to me, as if I stared into those eyes
in a thousand different lifetimes. Like our
souls had known each other all this time.

You forget about me like
an overdue library book
that sits collecting dust in
the back of your bookshelf

Don't text them tonight.

When its 3AM, and you're all alone with your thoughts thinking about the good and bad times, don't text them.

Don't get on their social media page to see if they found someone new.
Don't scroll through old texts or re-read notes from months ago trying to figure out where it went wrong.
Don't listen to those songs they sent you on repeat or look through old photos to remember cute moments you had.
Just don't do it to yourself.

I know it hurts.
Probably more and more every day.
But we can't go back in time.
So, you need to learn to be okay with this broken heart for a little while longer until it heals, because it will.

So, if you were looking for a reason to text them, take these words as a sign to not do it.

Close your eyes, take a deep breath, and remember who you are.

Losing you hurt, and it didn't just happen overnight.
I lost a little piece of you every day until there was nothing else to hold onto.
Yeah, losing you hurt.
It's the type of hurt I don't think you come back from.

Everyone has the
potential to leave you
but you can't leave you
so it's important to
love you most

I want to know the sound of your heartbeat
as if it's a song I've played a thousand times

There are a trillion stars in the galaxies,
and she's still shining brighter

I don't know what it is about you.
Maybe it's the way nothing else matters
when we are together or how you make me
smile more than anyone else has.
It could be the way you say the right things
at the right time. But whatever it is, I can't
seem to get enough of it. I just want you to
know it means everything to me

BREAKFAST

It was early morning and you felt as if the
rest of the world was still asleep.

You sat there with the crisp air on your face
pondering thoughts so wildly captivating.

And as you listened to the birds singing
and the breeze rustling the leaves,

I swear I've never seen anything so
unexplainably beautiful

All of this, simply over breakfast.

SUNDAYS ARE FOR CUDDLES,
CARBS, AND TONS OF SEX

I wanted my lips
to kiss every inch of
your body

I'd watch as you
quivered with
anticipation to
where I'll go next

I was just someone
who got drunk
on the taste of you

Being Liked < Being Valued

COLD SHEETS

There's nothing but cold sheets in an
empty bed. The bed where we once held
each other close, now worlds apart.

The bed I still reach across to your side,
only to find imprints your body once filled.

So as I lay here, I acclimate to the
absence of you.

In these moments, I've never craved
anything more than your soul tangled
with mine in these cold sheets

You are so focused on
not losing them that
you forget to see that

you're losing yourself
in the process

Take a deep breath and remember
that it's okay to start over.
It's okay to give somebody else a
chance to <u>love you</u>

I need you to love your life.
I know that's asking a lot in the
world we live in.
But I need you to try.

Go somewhere new this weekend,
Take photos of everything,
Tell people you love them,
Get those shoes you've
always wanted
Do shit that scares you
because so many of us die
without truly living, and I don't
want you to be one of them.

Make your story the best one yet.

I THINK PARTS OF ME WILL
ALWAYS WANT YOU,
EVEN THE PARTS I KNOW THAT
CAN'T HAVE YOU

You moved on and truthfully it felt as
though I didn't exist in your world anymore.
No call, no text, no communication at all,
Just the stillness of my slowly beating heart.
It was months later when I heard the news
that you were happy with someone new.
As much as I wanted to hate you for it, I
couldn't. They say if you love someone it
means wanting them to be happy, even if
that happiness doesn't include you.
I guess I just always wondered if you took
him to all the places you took me, like your
favorite ice cream shop with the cute plastic
spoons, or the hill we would climb to see the
view of the city. It took me a while to grasp
the understanding that you can love
someone and let them go. I just needed to
learn that at my own speed. I needed to shift
the focus I had on you, to myself. For I had
to learn that being happy meant not focusing
on what you were doing anymore.

When they hurt you
let it hurt
and then
you must let it go

"You know one thing
I love about you?"
He said.

Everything

The universe has a weird way of
making things work out.

It's beautifully unpredictable

You told me to stop holding on to the
past as if I enjoy living there.
As if I enjoy reliving those moments
that shattered every atom of my essence
As if I enjoy watching my confidence
slowly deteriorate right in front of me.

I didn't need you to criticize my trauma,
I just needed you to be my safe place,
my home for when the storm started to
rage within my chest.

Love travels at its own speed so do not rush in

or wish it would find you faster

because we never really have a choice anyway

Sometimes
it is much easier being alone.
At least no one can hurt me here
but me

I have done a lot of things wrong in my life
and I don't want loving you to be one of them,
so if I can get one thing right
I want it to be <u>you</u>

Dear Mind,

I am in a constant battle with you.
It is tug of war that I seem to lose every
time. I think it is time I take my power
back now. I think it is time I win.

Love,
The Heart

After all this time:

I should have known you weren't capable
of loving me.
I should have known you weren't how my
story ends.
I should have known your hands were too
weak to hold my heart.
I should have known better.
I should have done better.
It was a mistake for putting too much trust
in you

The boy asked:
"What is love?"

The old man replied:
"Love is listening to smooth jazz
while sipping on red wine
and slow dancing in the kitchen
cooking your favorite meal with her"

She is soft yet strong
Vulnerable yet reserved
Broken yet so unbelievably wholesome
She is everything anyone could ask for
She is the type of girl you go to war beside
The type of girl you stay with forever.

SOMEDAYS I DON'T
KNOW IF I BELIEVE
IN A HIGHER POWER,
BUT IF HEAVEN
WERE A REAL PLACE,
IT WOULD BE
WHENEVER YOU'RE
IN MY ARMS

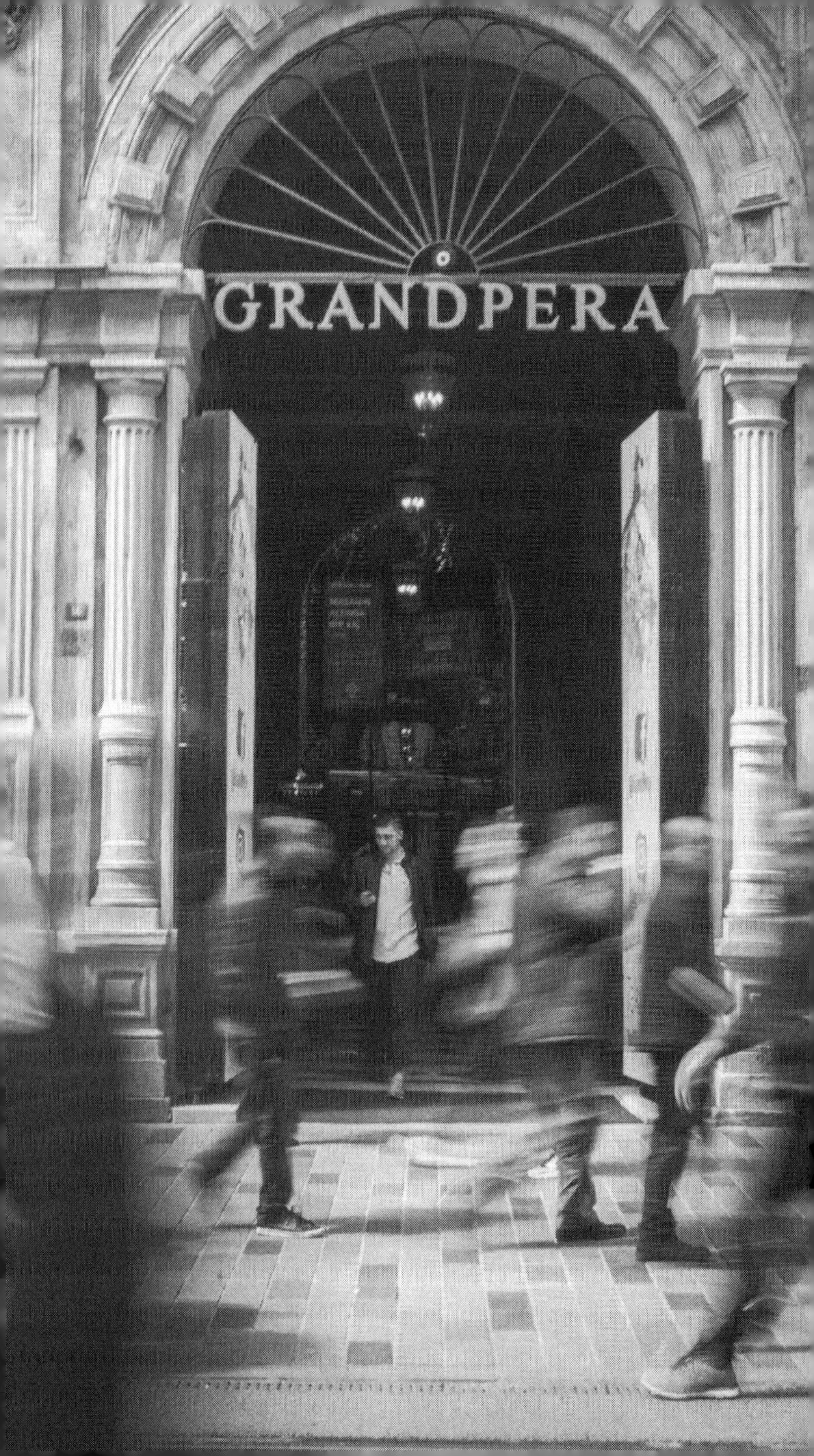
GRANDPERA

And if you decide to leave me
Please take all of me with you
For I don't want to walk this earth knowing
that half of me will always be looking for
the other half of you

We pretend to be okay
so we don't have to admit
just how not okay we really are

The moment you realize that you're in control of your own life… Is the same moment you become unstoppable

She spent forever building walls around her
heart so that no one could get in to hurt her
But the higher she built,
the harder it became for someone to
make her happy

She was my perfect dose of serotonin.
and I was her favorite shot of dopamine

I want that
carve our initials in a tree
type of *love*

I knew you would be the one to hurt me.
I knew it in the moment we met,
but I still didn't care.

I didn't mind that you would break me into a
million little pieces
and scatter them anywhere but here like
debris along the highway.

I know it would happen all along
and I've just been waiting, just collecting
piece after piece trying to put myself back
together again because I don't recognize
myself anymore.

I don't believe diamond nor steel is the
strongest object on earth,
For the human heart even after it has been
battered and bruised still beats.

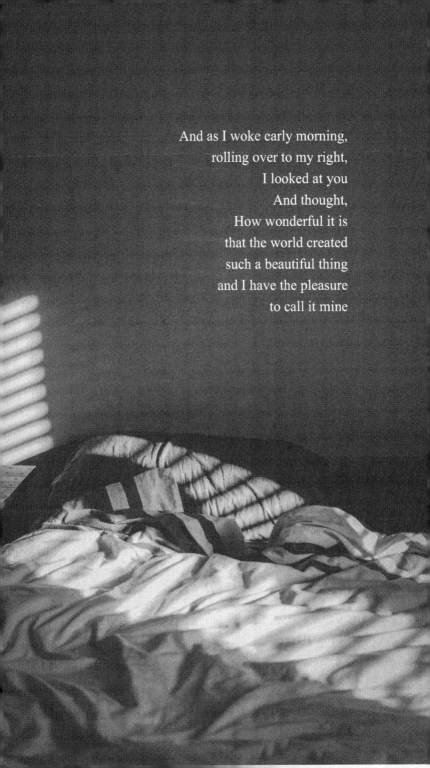

And as I woke early morning,
rolling over to my right,
I looked at you
And thought,
How wonderful it is
that the world created
such a beautiful thing
and I have the pleasure
to call it mine

SHE
WEARS
HER
SCARS
LIKE
BADGES
FROM
THE
LOVERS
BEFORE

She's only 25
And carries the weight of the world on her shoulders
She's been through so much trauma in her life but
never lets it alter who she wants to be.
She has flaws that make her beautiful
But only sees it as misfortune
But on the days where she can't seem to tuck away
the insecurities and they slowly start to consume her
That's when she will need you most
Don't speak, don't leave, just be.

She had fire in her eyes
and was covered in tattoos
If the devil had a favorite
I'm sure it'd be you

You can learn so much
about someone in the silence.

Just lying there with the dim streetlights
casting shadows on your ceiling
and nothing but the sound of rushing cars
on the freeway just outside your window.

Just two souls fluent in silence

For the silence will teach you a deeper
truth than words ever could.

I long for the days
where it feels like I'm not falling apart.
The days where I'm not staring at myself in the
mirror with tears flooding my face trying to convince
the one staring back at me to not give up.
I long for the days

Last
night I talked to the
moon about you
I told it
all my secrets
& confessions.
Like how I can
feel your warmth
without evening
touching you,
like how in a
crowded place
my eyes always
seem to find
yours, or how the
world   could be
crumbling down
and you   would
still find a   way
to bloom so
beautifully.

It was a beautiful night in Paris.
One they will remember forever.
As they walked the cobble streets drunk,
talking about the universe and all within,
sipping on whiskey from the bottle
he couldn't help to smile as the moon slowly
danced on her skin.

You're a breath of fresh air, you're
the first beam of morning light
seeping through the window blinds,
you're a warm hug tightly wrapped
around the body,

you're all good things.

I hope one day we find each other again.
Maybe when we are older and our lives are
less chaotic
We'll laugh about how we almost made it
but just fell short.

And I'll tell you all the things I should
have said when I had you.
Like all the notes I wrote you but
crinkled up and threw away
Or how you were all my hearted wanted

But that day isn't today.
Today we just don't fit and I can't pretend
that we do

But there will always be a part of me
hoping you still search for me in a sky
full of stars

I hope you say my name when
you are talking to him.
I hope you think of me when he's
touching your skin.
I hope you lose your thoughts
because I'm what's on your mind.
I hope you never know this
feeling of being left behind.

And I think I am just a guy
who walks this earth
with a permanently broken heart

I shouldn't have called you up but I'm not
good at moving on.

So while I have you on the line
Tell me I'm not the only one who's afraid
to be lonely